Wood Pool

(A Carp Water)

Wood Pool

(A Carp Water)

"BB"

Illustrated by

D.J. Watkins Pitchford

MMXI • THE MEDLAR PRESS • ELLESMERE

Published by The Medlar Press Limited,
The Grange, Ellesmere, Shropshire.

ISBN 978-1-907110-22-1

A limited edition of this book was published by the Medlar Press in 1996.

This edition is based on an original copy once owned by the author and containing ten extra drawings.

Typeset in 12 on 15 point Garamond Roman.
Produced in England by The Medlar Press Limited, Ellesmere, England.

Contents

"BB"

Denys James Watkins-Pitchford

Born Lamport, Northamptonshire 25th July 1905, died Sudborough 8th September 1990

Denys was brought up in comfortably Edwardian circumstances with his two brothers by their mother, Edith Elizabeth Wilson, and his father Walter, who was a vicar. Denys, thought to be 'delicate' as a child, was educated privately, which in his case really meant that, because he never went to school, being taught instead at home by a governess, his father and a local schoolmaster. His parents were musical, but emotionally distant and neither of them shared his love of the outdoors and so, constantly troubled by childhood illness, Denys lived in a small, almost hermetically sealed world which cast its eyes longingly back to another age; this had a profound effect on his character and his writing. His twin brother Roger, on the other hand, had a very different experience of life and was sent to boarding school, emigrating to Canada when he was in his early twenties.

Denys spent much of his spare time exploring the surrounding countryside, where he developed a tremendous love of nature as well as a passion for shooting and fishing. His parents were very class-conscious which, combined with the way he was educated, meant that he had little contact with other children and was taught to fish by local men like Job Perkins. Given his upbringing, it isn't surprising that Denys was socially awkward and he simultaneously valued and feared solitude; a contradiction which he spent a lifetime trying to resolve and accounted for his reserved character.

At fifteen, having failed to excel at anything in particular during his studies, Denys started a course at Northampton Art College, which came as a shock given his natural shyness, but although the course was very traditional, he developed an interest in scraperboard while he was there and managed to win a scholarship to Paris. In 1926, he went to the Royal College of Art, where he finally managed to get to grips with the world beyond the comforting fields of his home, although he still longed to return and he painted and drew birds and animals constantly in his spare time.

When he left the College in 1928, Watkins-Pitchford found himself at something of a loss about what to do, but after spending an entire summer fishing and shooting, he decided to become a schoolteacher. After weathering the General Strike, the grapevine brought him news of an assistant arts mastership at Rugby School, for which he successfully applied. Although teaching was hardly a vocation as far as Denys was concerned, it was an environment he understood and, when it boiled down to it, he was often more comfortable in the company of the boys than he was with adults, not that he would have volunteered for it. He stayed at Rugby for seventeen years, only leaving after the war's end.

Watkins-Pitchford started writing not long after he took up his post at the school, particularly for the *Shooting Times* - by then he had a fair amount of experience of goose shooting, in addition to his growing skill as a coarse fisherman. Then, in 1938, he had two manuscripts accepted (*The Sportsman's Bedside Book* and *Wild Lone, The Story of a Pytchley Fox*) and he began to appreciate that there might be a way to lead the life he had always dreamed about; so he set about writing with a will. He married Cecily Mary Adnitt in 1939, by whom he had a son, Robin and a daughter, Angela; sadly his son died aged only seven and his wife predeceased him by sixteen years.

In 1942, Watkins-Pitchford won the Carnegie medal for *Little Grey Men* and a light began to glimmer at the end of the tunnel; although he struggled to make ends meet until the end of the Sixties, an impressive stream of titles followed, at the rate of nearly one a year for the next three decades. He wrote all his books (apart from *Be Quiet and Go A-Angling*) under the pseudonym "BB", which was taken from a shotgun load used to bring down geese, and illustrated most of them using scraperboard, which prior to his use of the method had rarely been used outside advertising. He also contributed regular pieces to *The Field* and *Country Life*, becoming an icon of British sporting writing in the process, although this was only truly the case by the Eighties, by which time he was writing much less and was having regular haemodialysis.

"BB" wrote some fine fishing books, including *Be Quiet and Go A-Angling* (1949), *Wood Pool* (1958), and *The Whopper* (1967). *Be Quiet* was originally published using the pseudonym Michael Traherne, something "BB" later regretted and in 1987 he updated the book, published it under his own name "BB" and changed the title to *A Fisherman's Folly. Confessions of a Carp Fisher*, published in 1950, became a classic, partly for the quality of the writing, but also because it was the first book to identify carp fishers as a clan. When he wrote it, the record stood at twenty-six pounds; barely a year later, "BB" found himself sitting beside the carp lake at Woldale, in the company of his friends Richard Walker and Maurice Ingham, discussing why carp fishing wasn't more popular. From this conversation, the Carp Catchers' Club evolved. "BB"s involvement was ironic in a way, given that he fished for much the same reason that he shot - it was just a good excuse to be out enjoying the countryside. From that conversation, today's specimen carp fishing movement is descended and yet many of the people involved are unaware of the role "BB" played.

Andrew Herd

Introduction

After "BB" had published *Confessions of a Carp Fisher* in 1950 - a book dense with intensely felt atmosphere and drama - it seemed a logical step for him to have then written this much quieter, more contemplative book about his favourite angling subjects. In his clear, straightforward prose style, "BB" describes the creation of a dream and the end of a quest that had begun with *Confessions.* He had always been searching for his ideal carp water and in *Wood Pool* he writes about a lovely old Northampton pond and how, by careful stocking with the same strain of carp that originally seeded Redmire, he transformed it into a carp fisher's paradise. He describes the gradual changes of the seasons, the progress of the fish, the feelings he has for his pool as the carp put a new spirit into it. Then - at last - he casts . . .

"BB" was a great admirer of Thoreau's classic *Walden Pond* and he would, I think, have secretly liked to have written something in the same vein. Yet he was both too modest and too concerned with all the fine detail of natural life and with fisherman's dreams to have attempted something more universal. He was content to leave us *Wood Pool* as a kind of alternative *Walden* - a smaller scale, very English vision.

Chris Yates, July 1996

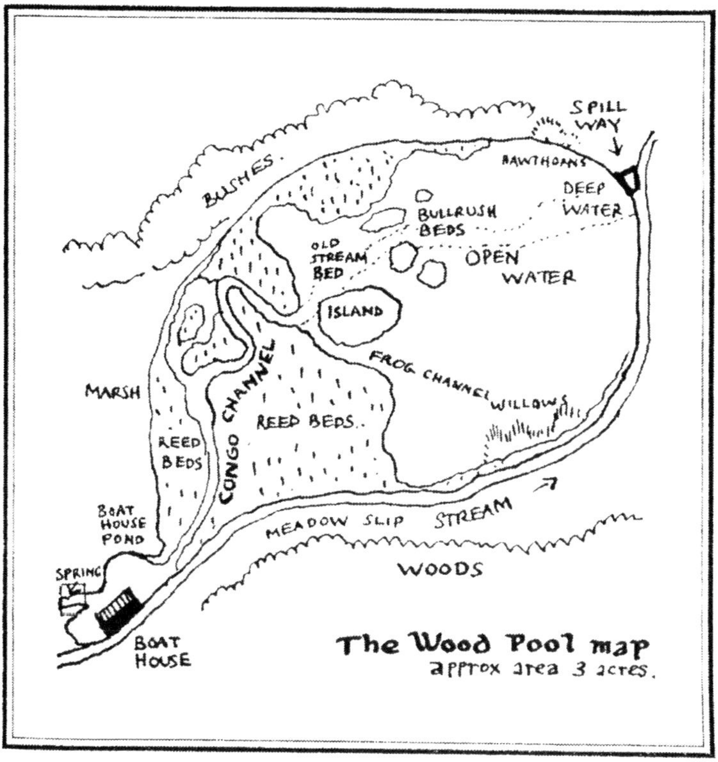
SPILL WAY
BUSHES
HAWTHORNS
DEEP WATER
BULLRUSH BEDS
OLD STREAM BED
OPEN WATER
ISLAND
FROG CHANNEL
WILLOWS
CONGO CHANNEL
MARSH
REED BEDS
REED BEDS
BOAT HOUSE POND
SPRING
MEADOW SLIP STREAM
WOODS
BOAT HOUSE
The Wood Pool map
approx area 3 acres.

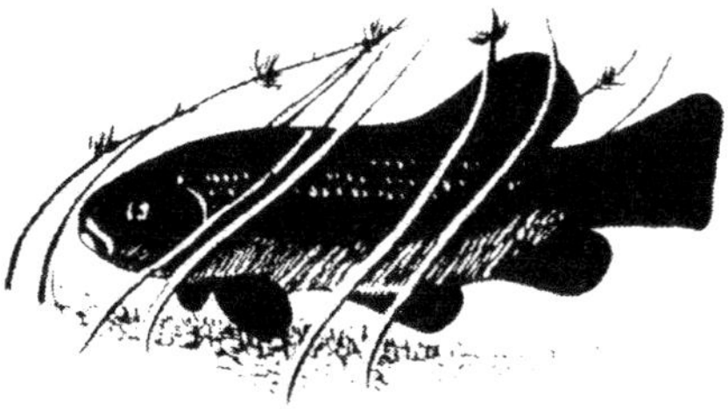

CHAPTER ONE

The Way to the Water

The way to the water is hot walking for I begin this portrait of the pool in June. It is a meandering path no wider than a sheep track, which winds across the old ironstone workings. Since most of the rabbits have gone, the infant brambles, bootlace-size, have sprung up everywhere; they catch the ankles and are so tough they can trip the unwary.

The grass that hides them is coarse and long, green now, but at summer's end it is a tawny buff; 'lion grass' I call it, for it is tall enough to conceal a crouching lion, and is of the same colour. The pheasants love it, so do the woodcock in the early winter dusks when the Hunter's Moon rises over the parkland woods and the thoughts of greylags on lonely northern firths make me as restless as any old wild goose.

This wild tract of land is now grown up with dense thickets of blackthorn where once the rabbits harboured. Many a winter's afternoon I have hunted them out with my springer spaniel Patsy, and very sporting shots they were, darting from thicket to thicket, some of the most difficult marks you could find.

Away over the tumbled ground my path leads on until it dips down into the deep trench where once a railway carried the orange-stained ironstone trucks. The bottom of this trench is flattened, you may still see the rotting sleepers embedded in the white chalky soil.

Here the navvies walked the tight-rope planks, wheeling their loaded barrows, long before the days of mechanical grabbers. How those slender planks swung up and down! Sometimes, a man new to the game, poised high above the chasm would make one false step and the weighty barrow's iron-shod wheel would slip over the plank's edge carrying the man with it.

Walking now over this hot and rough terrain how one longs for the water! But we are not there yet. The heated air beats up from the chalk hitting one as heat strikes from a pavement, but more gently tempered. It smells of bleached hot hay. Mick, my black retriever, follows at my heels, panting, his lungs working like bellows: the flies hum continuously. At last we reach the tall black poplars which give the first hint of water. The smallest zephyr of summer breeze sets their heart-shaped leaves a-wag, the sound is cool and restful on this hot day.

Beyond the poplars is the fir wood. This was planted some forty years ago. The trees, growing close together, shut out the light, and stepping from the hot grass-covered workings into the black shade is like entering a cellar. There is a sweet scent of pines, the footsteps on the needles are noiseless, one might be walking on a thick pile carpet. Shafts of sunlight pierce the gloomy scented shadows, glowing with golden red coins of light on the needles underneath. Ahead, a silvery golden brightness shows where the wood ends and the spires of rose bay rise up in a slender forest. They are already knotting into bud and there are yellow flowerets on the elder just beyond.

Here is an open space of rough grass and a line of old oak trees heavy in leaf, a favourite perching place for the wood pigeons in the winter afternoons. They come there to rest awhile before flying the short distance across to the fir wood.

This summer's morning the mounds of sunlit foliage are unstirred by any breeze. A few purple hairstreaks are flitting around the high trusses. This beautiful little butterfly, so alike in many ways to its lordly relation the rare purple emperor butterfly, is quite common in this corner of the wood.

Under the tree is the old pump-house. This once housed the machinery which pumped the water up to the 'big house' in the park but it has not been used for a quarter of a century. The plant is still there, the massive fly-wheels and rusting engine. Bats sleep among the rafters and the dark little interior is as silent and dust-laden as some neglected vault. But the exterior is charming to the eye, it has a sort of Izaak Walton air about it and might easily be mistaken for a fishing hut.

The nearness of the water is now evident. From beyond a dense palisade of alders which fringe the brook come the sounds of water-fowl, the conversational *quoit quoit* of coots and sharp *cruik* of moorhens. The distant sound of coots *quoiting* brings instantly to my mind the great attraction of still water. It is a strange sound which carries for a considerable distance and is one of the most familiar to the coarse fisherman. It is only uttered when the birds are content and it is in no sense an alarm note. I have heard bulb horns on boys' bicycles make the exact sound.

I can smell the water now, a faint scent which has something of the sea in it, yet is quite distinctive. Most old pools have this smell. There is a hint of rotting leaves in it, a half-sweet, half-rotten perfume which is very pleasing.

I go past the pump-house, run down into the dry trench which was once the bed of the stream which fed the engine, and climb carefully under the barbed wire, taking care not to catch the cover of my rod bag on the sharp spines. Then I am in the meadow and the sunlight where the meadow-sweet is knee high and already in flower.

Meadow-sweet and water go together. It is a short way across this little pasture and still no sight of the· pool. Ahead is a huge clump of willows and ash trees, a plank bridge which crosses the brook, and beyond at last can be glimpsed the tarred timbers of the boat-house roof. This marks the beginning of all my fishing voyages, this is where I take everyone when they come with me to see the pool.

I must now ask the reader to look at the map of the pool and its environs. Even when we reach the boat-house we cannot see the main pool. This lies to the right beyond the island and the reed beds. The brook which I am now crossing by way of the plank bridge, rises some three miles away. Here, where it runs through the estate, it is large enough to hold trout and I hope one day to stock it. I have caught trout up to 3lb in weight in brooks no bigger than this, and it has nice holding pools, plenty of weed and shingly shallows where no doubt brook trout would breed freely.

As will be seen by the map, the brook runs all down the southern bank, turning sharply to the left at the end of the lake where it passes along the base of the artificial embankment. Because it is liable to heavy spates it was not utilised to feed the lake.

My feet ring hollowly on the wooden plank. Mick the labrador, who unlike my other dogs will never walk across, plunges down the steep sandy bank into the water and stays awhile in mid stream shaking himself all over. He loves the water.

Three years ago some wild bees built their nest on the underside of the plank. The nest hung down like the white udder of a cow. Woe betide anyone who attempted to cross the bridge! At the first echoing, vibrating, footfall the bees emerged in an angry, buzzing swarm. I took a photograph of this nest and sent it to *Country Life* who published it. I cannot think now why we never took the swarm, it was a wonderful opportunity, but I fear bee stings and the bees know it.

Once over the bridge I turn left and follow the track on the top of the bank towards the boat-house. On the right of this narrow scythed track is a thick belt of reed mace. Beyond that is a narrow channel of water which I call Congo Channel. This winds away through dense reed beds to the open lake. On the far side are more reeds, then a narrow strip of marshy meadow grown with sedge, pink with that marsh-loving plant which delights in damp places, the lady's smock. Its other names are milkmaids or cuckoo flower, country names but very apt.

In a few yards I reach the boat-house, the harbour from which all my voyages have their beginnings and their end. Here, the narrow channel which gives access to the lake widens out into a fair-sized pond which is of some depth, and bottomed with thick mud.

An old poaching fellow once told me that years ago he shot a mallard at this spot and went in after it. He went too far and sank in the mud. It took him an hour to get out. I don't often see mallard at this corner of the lake because they are shy of the boat-house . But in hard weather when the lake is frozen solid there is always open water just here, for the powerful spring which feeds the lake rises a few yards away in a small hollow, fenced round with park railings.

I remember one brilliant frosty winter's morning, when everything was as sparkling and bright as a diamond, stalking up under cover of the reed mace and seeing fifteen or twenty mallard splashing and preening around the spring, a beautiful picture which would have delighted Thorburn. The whole of the lake was frozen hard and so was the channel through the reeds; only at that spot was there any open water.

We never shoot the mallard, as the lake and its environs we regard as a bird sanctuary. The only birds which I shoot there are the wood pigeons in the winter months when they come in to sleep in the firs.

Here then is the boat-house, tarred and black, double padlocked, fenced about with barbed wire as it well needs to be. Boat-houses have a dreadful fascination for small boys (and big ones too; indeed, it is the older boys that do the damage). When we first came here the boat-house had no proper door, only a flimsy thing of pine pales nailed to cross-battens. This was beaten in every summer by louts until I found in my cellar a stout door of oak which luckily just fitted the opening. I put this in place and fastened it with a hasp and padlock. The padlock was broken and ripped out within a week. I then bored two holes in the oak door about 2 feet apart and passed chains through and round the main timbers of the house and secured them with really big padlocks.

Mischievous boys who found they could not break the padlocks next forced a way round the entrance by wading in the water which unfortunately is not more than a couple of feet just there. We procured rolls of concertina wire and placed it against the side of the entrance, well into the lake and in addition I barricaded the side with something just as formidable, a cut-down hawthorn bush which was so heavy that I had a job to put it into position.

This formed a sort of *Boma* such as hunters in Africa erect round their camping places. So far this has kept the louts at bay.

A mass of thorns is a wonderful protection; you can't climb through like you can with barbed wire, and once the reeds grow up among the branches it anchors the thorns in place. Not even a 14-year-old schoolboy will face it, and that is saying a good deal.

The rods and gear are placed in the boat and the padlock removed, for I always keep a lock on the boat as well as upon the door. Mick enters the boat gingerly; like all dogs he distrusts the uneasy motion, and has never got used to it.

Gently I push against the wooden floor of the staging and we glide out into the open water and the warm air. After the gloom of the boat-house the sunlight dazzles the eyes. I push on down the narrow channel I have cut through the reeds. There seems no air at all. The water in the channel is so shallow that the keel of the boat catches from time to time. Were it not for the mud you could wade almost out to the main lake.

Arrowing furls of water chase away ahead of the boat. These are caused by small carp and tench which venture down this channel in hot weather. You can mark their course by the arrow-headed ripples as each fish makes off for the deeper water.

On either side rise the tall reeds which give no shade and shut out the breeze. Before long the tops of the trees on the island glide into view. After devious twists and turns (the stranger needs a pilot for this tortuous channel) we emerge into a series of rushy pools beloved of the bigger fish on quiet summer evenings. The water is much deeper here, 4 feet and more, and as the boat glides on it deepens all the time.

Mallard rise up with a great bustle of wings. At last Congo Channel is behind us. We are in the throat of the lake, hard by the island itself. As we look along under the drooping boughs, the faintly shimmering expanse of the main lake dances and gleams. Drifts of white water daisy give the surface a frosted appearance. This is a tiresome weed but it soon dies down and, whilst it blooms, it gives fine food and shelter for fish. Indeed, I have seen the large carp browsing on it like cattle in a buttercup meadow.

A few more strokes of the oars and we have arrived at my favourite fishing pitch, a dense clump of reed mace in the centre of the lake.

How strange it is to think that only a few years back this was a silent forsaken water, untenanted by any fish save eels and stickle-backs!

How I stocked it must be left to the next chapter.

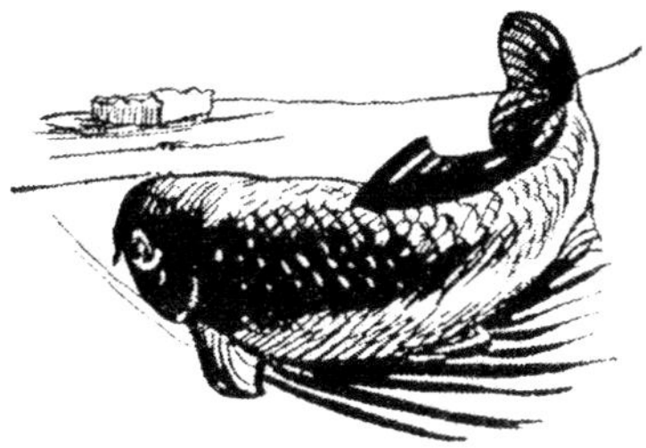

CHAPTER TWO

Stocking the Wood Pool

I picked up my can of fish from Kettering station on 2nd November, 1951, a gloomy afternoon with fog. They had travelled from Haslemere, one hundred mirror and common carp, mixed, and fifty tench. I peered into the round can which was shaped like a squat oast-house. The small fish, they appeared coal black, were about 3 inches long. They reminded me of a swarm of tadpoles.

It was dusk by the time I drove the Landrover into the stable yard and let fresh water into the can. The fish seemed lively enough, as fresh as paint.

Just as it grew dark I arrived with my heavy can on the bank of the Wood Pool. Thick vapour lay over the water muffling it in a milky fog. Mallard were quacking from the reeds beyond the island. Some were already flighting off. For me this was a big moment. A pool which had for so long been devoid of fish, inhabited only by beetles and eels, was to come to life again, to awaken in the sultry heats of summer to the splash of jumping fish. I waded in until the water was up to the top of my waders, then I gently submerged the can, tipping it a little sideways.

It was so dark I could only see the crinkle in the water as the inchlings left in a flurry. I peered again into the can. There were still about twenty little fish milling about in the bottom. I took them round to the spillway end where the water was deepest and let them free there. Nothing was left in the can; I put my hand in and felt round the cold, damp, interior.

Out there under the darkling water the carplings and tenchlings were free in a new wide world. I was not to see them again until nearly midsummer of the following year.

The fog thickened, owls called from the fir wood, summer seemed a world away.

* * *

In the spring of 1952 I was on the look-out for the carp. On sunny days I rowed all over the pool but saw not a single fish. Where had they gone? I had noticed no herons near the pool. Nothing was noted until mid-May when a farmer's boy, who had permission to fish for eels, caught two mirror carp on worm. He brought them up to the house in great excitement. I had said nothing about stocking the pool - once the news leaked out poachers would get to hear of it and however well one may police a pond, there are times when the sneak-poacher can have an hour or two - but I had to tell him how they came to be there.

These two mirror carp were so large I could not credit they were of my original stocking. Each was in fine condition, thick across the back and weighed about a pound apiece. That such rate of growth could have taken place in six months was beyond all belief. Evidently there was an ample food supply, and, like trout in a virgin water, the carp had put on weight at a great pace.*

As soon as we had a spell of warm weather I was on the watch for the rest of the fish; the farmer's boy had reported hundreds swimming by the spillway. And very soon I saw several big shoals passing, ten to twenty in a shoal, all much the same size as the two which had been caught.

On the right of the spillway, where the white may bush leans out over the pool, the water is in sunlight for the greater part of the day. This was a favourite basking spot for the carp. All during the rest of the summer when the weather was suitable, I saw them - motionless bars hanging in the amber water under the may bush.

One evening in September when I was walking along my cleared path towards the boat-house I came upon the half-eaten remains of a carp with the back bitten out. It was a fish of about a pound and a half in weight, obviously the work of a marauding otter. I was uneasy.

I knew that from time to time otters come up the brook, and it was what I had feared all along. D. F. Leney of the Surrey Trout Farm, Haslemere, wrote and told me that I should try to catch the poachers. He had lost the entire stock of a carp breeding pond through the attentions of an otter.

* *The facts of the stocking are as follows. On 2nd November, 1951 I put in one hundred mixed mirror and common carp and fifty tench. These were all 3-4 inch fish. In November 1953, I added a further fifty mixed carp of the same size. Now as to growth: two mirrors from the original stocking were caught in May 1952, and weighed 1lb apiece. In 1956-7 numerous 5-6lb carp were caught (with tench up to 3lb). The biggest fish to date is a common carp of 14lb 10oz caught in June 1957.*

They are wary creatures and I had no suitable trap. Apart from that, I love otters, even when I know they are taking my fish, and I could not bring myself to try to trap him. I did however take the gun along some nights but I never saw or heard him.

Then a labourer on his Sunday walk, with a dog along the brook just beside the pool, surprised a large otter in a stickle. The terrier with him leapt in at once and killed it. When I heard about it I was glad for I was sure the creature was the one working on my stock. The trouble with an otter is that he will go for the big fish and leave the small ones as beneath his notice. Wholesale killing only takes place (so we are told) when otters are teaching their cubs to fish.

The wandering otter (they are great gypsies), may take one or two fish but will not usually stay more than a day or so, even on a well-stocked lake, if it is far from its holt.

I looked for the tench that summer of 1952 but never saw one. Later I was to regret putting in so many. They are prolific breeders and do not show themselves as readily as carp.

In late autumn, on warm afternoons when I was strolling around with the gun, I would often stand on my favourite spot under the willows and look out across the still pool. The island limes were yellowing, the birches too, dropping their pale leaves into the tawny water. Occasionally I saw a carp jump over by the bulrush beds and along the sedgy margin where the cattle come to drink and the wild water mint scents the air.

The pool was becoming 'alive' for me, my fish were still there, but I would have to wait another three years before they would be old enough to breed, or be worthy of my steel.

During this slack time I found there was plenty to occupy

me. The summer's growth of brambles had to be cut back again and the boundary trees still needed attention, for the wych elm's branches were hanging low over the path, and two leaks had appeared in the bank which gave me cause for anxiety. The dam by the boat-house was 'weeping' a little. It was very difficult to find where the water was getting through. Water rats had driven their tunnels in the soft mud inside the boat-house, about 6 inches below the water level, and one of these must have penetrated the bank. Also I noticed that the ground close to my repair dam was soft and spongy; this had to be rammed down and fresh turves added.

Much of the nuisance of this leakage was caused by the original design of the lake. To have a deepish brook washing the artificial bank all down one side was asking for trouble. It is impossible to prevent water rats, and even rabbits, from burrowing into an artificial bank. Once the water finds its way through, even a small hole like that of a rat's burrow, then the pressure of water behind will enlarge it. One stands the risk of the whole bank going. Some twenty years ago the artificial dam at the eastern end broke in a heavy flood. The water rushed through making a wide breach and swept down the valley to some workmen's cottages a mile distant where some pigs were drowned, and the inhabitants of the cottages were marooned in their upper rooms for some hours. This incident is still remembered and talked about in the ale house of the district, even though it happened many years ago. The fact that pigs were drowned seemed to have made a very deep impression.

I could not trace this leak from the inside of the boat-house. I then tried to trace it back from the outside. This too was unsuccessful. I was afraid of weakening the bank so I plugged the cavity as far up as I was able with clay and rammed more turves on top, a temporary job but efficient while it lasted. The other leak was by the spillway. I noticed water appearing half-way down the stone spill, and searching about among the mud and weeds by the fish grill above, I found a small hole, again obviously a rat hole, close to the concrete work and going down vertically. This was easily plugged with clay. The leak was stopped at once.

Artificial lakes where there is a dam always give trouble unless the banks are made with a thick inner core of concrete; even then the water has a way of burrowing round.

Quite early in the spring of 1953 I saw the carp again. I came upon a dead one, with its tail bitten off, lying on the path between the dam and the boat-house , probably the work of a heron. It was a fish of about 3lb. There was no sign of any other fish. I went out in the punt and searched carefully over the whole water, which was very clear. I could see the bottom everywhere save in the deepest part by the spillway. There was no weed for fish to hide in. All I could see were the grooved marks of eels in the mud. One would not think it possible for fish to hide themselves so well but carp lie quiescent during the cold months, burying themselves deep in the mud, and do not begin to stir until the water temperature rises in April. Even then they are not very active and do not really begin to show themselves until the spawning season in May and early June. So if you stock a pool with carp and tench, give them time to show themselves. In my ignorance I was sure that otters had killed the lot, assisted by herons, and I there and then placed another order with the Surrey Trout Farm for another fifty common and mirror carp. As it turned out I need not have worried. The carp were there all right, in the mud and among the thick weeds.

As soon as the warm weather came, and the weed growth showed on top, fish were moving all over the lake.

CHAPTER THREE

Carp Weather

Today the upraised tails of cattle, each waving a hairy plume, are bobbing under the lime trees like the pennants on knights' lances. The limes up in the park perfume the air magically; the last, loveliest wild perfume of summer.

This, my friends, is real carp and tench weather. Always associated in my mind with the fragrance of the limes are these still waters of the Wood Pool cooling after the heat of the day. The carp have been lazy and listless all through the scorching hours. They have lain lolling, true sun worshippers, barely an inch under the surface, warming themselves like cats at fires. Sometimes as I have sat under the big willow by the spillway in the green coolness of its shadow I have seen a shining massive back appear stealthily like the back of a 'blowing' whale.

Twenty yards from the spillway, in the deepest part of the pool, there is a bed of water plantain, tough weed and an enemy of gut and hooks. Its narrow, willow-shaped leaves are like spread fingers. It is among these that the very big carp like to bask on hot days such as this.

When seen from behind and end-on the big fish always appear to have a list to starboard, one rarely sees them on an even keel. They seem to lean on the water, sideways, like fat men lolling in armchairs. As the shining back slowly appears (smooth black skin without any pattern of scales) one knows it is one of the big scaleless or leather carp from the original stocking. Often there are one or two more patriarchs sunning close by, and, if you wait long enough, a netted back appears, clad in mail, each bronze scale lapped beautifully over the other. How much more attractive are these full-scaled carp! The scaleless mirrors I often think repugnant, even when they have a rich mahogany hue along the sides. But scaleless or not, they are noble fighters and excessively wary.

On hot summer mornings I have tried to interest them in floating crusts, for this is one of the most exciting forms of carp fishing. You strike as the fish bolts with the bread, timing your stroke with the nicety of a heron.

The dry crust is cast forth. It lands with a light splash among the water plantain leaves; it appears white in the full sunlight, as white as the feather of a swan. Immediately there are a series of swirls as the big fellows dive in alarm. The spinning whorls of water, miniature whirlpools, move sideways from the point where the big bodies were propelled downwards, and spin onwards into the green sedge blades.

A big carp can do a wonderful crash dive. It puts its head down and closes its fins and gives one almighty sweep with its tail.

I wait quietly under the willow tree. The little blue

damoselle dragonflies, which are always flitting about the green rushes of the spillway on hot days, go dancing in airy flight over the pool. Some settle as delicately as thistledown on the flower spikes of the plantain. Shiny beetles, shaped like dodgem cars, whirl about. They are called 'rotifors' and seem to lead a busy life. No doubt the fish take them when they can, for the rotifor seems to be able to dive as easily as a big carp if alarmed.

In a few moments you see a stir in the water a little way beyond the floating crust. It is a movement which is instantly betraying, the same that I see when fishing at edge of dark from by the island. These are not ever-widening circular ripples such as are made from a stone cast into a still surface, they seem to be ripple bars which swirl outwards and never take on a circular shape, more like the ripples caused by the passage of a boat.

Out under the water plantain leaves you may see through your polarised glasses the shadowy dim shape of a grey-blue dirigible. It is one of the mirrors and must weigh well into double figures. This is undoubtedly one of the few survivors of the original stocking in 1951. I may be quite in error, for of course it is very hard to say exactly what fish you have in a three-acre pool, much of it grown up with weed, but I have never seen more than ten of the 'whoppers' at any one time. Perhaps the others were taken by otters or herons, though I do not think the latter would tackle a carp over 10lb. Perhaps I am wrong. I have found a big fish of about 10lb with its tail gone, but I suspected an otter.

Watch this great fish carefully for you may learn much of the way a carp inspects a suspicious object. It can see the crust above it in its circular window, which is the fish's area of vision. Maybe, too, it can smell it. But it is far too cunning to take it straight away, or even to approach the bait. The fish swims round slowly with an occasional powerful thrust of its tail. All the time its large gold and brown eye is fixed on the white crust which revolves slowly as the passage of the fish below disturbs the surface.

This circling may continue for quite five minutes. It will swim slowly around with dignified mien or maybe another fish will come along, attracted by its circling companion. If that occurs then one or other will most likely have a grab at the bread. If, however, the original finder is undisturbed he will slowly swim up to the bread and pause a second. There is a noise like the cork being pulled from a champagne bottle, and the bread may (or may not) disappear. If the carp has missed his grab, or thought better of it in the last split second, then the bread revolves rapidly and often disintegrates, which is exactly what our wily customer would like to have happen, for he can devour the sinking remnants at leisure. Or the fish may take the bread into his mouth. If he does so he will immediately dive with it, and as he dives he either swallows the morsel or spits it out, when it bobs up to the top again. The big carp in the Wood Pool do not take kindly to bread, possibly because they have not been educated to it.

This business of educating them to a chosen bait is quite important. I have fished in pools where no fish will look at a worm but will take only paste. In others the recognised bait is potato - it is specially so in Lincolnshire carp ponds - and there is one fine carp water in the West Country, where they will look at nothing but floating bread. Carp become addicted to floating bread in waters where wild-fowl abound and are fed by hand.

There is a small private water in Norfolk where the stock of wild-fowl are fed by the keeper and as soon as the mash is cast in enormous tame carp which live in the broad come plunging round to share the feast.

How long is it before a carp takes a 'set' bait? I should say at least a couple of seasons. In a newly stocked water, worm is the safest bet; even in a bread or potato carp water I can't believe that a worm would be refused if the fish were really hungry. Carp eat a considerable quantity of vegetable matter such as duck weed, and it is highly probable that by so doing they also swallow, at the same time, minute forms of aquatic life. Young wild ducks delight in duck weed, not so much for the weed itself but for the insects it contains. Pick a lump of green American duck weed from a pond and examine it. You will not need a microscope to see the numberless creepy crawlies among its close green leaves.

On this sweltering June morning (we shall remember this June of 1957 with gratitude after so many weary wet summers) most of the carp are 'up on top'.

In the very centre of the Wood Pool, near where I planted a white water lily two years back (and which never grew as the swans pulled it up) there is a mass of water daisy weed. It is not attached to the bottom of the pond. This particular mass has been pulled up by the swans; it floats motionless in the sun-warmed water, like the floating seaweed islands of the Sargasso Sea. This large area of weed acts as a tent roof or gigantic parasol. All fish prefer to bask with some protection near, in the form of weeds, branches, or the shadow of a bridge. As I stand on the spillway looking out across the shining mirror I can see a fish stir from time to time and a shining back heaves up and disappears from sight. They rarely jump during these blazing hours, that activity will come later. Exactly *why* carp jump remains rather a mystery. In some carp waters they do not jump at all.

There was a pond in Devon, quite a small one, where I never saw a carp jump. The inhabitants of the pond were lean common 'monastic' type (true wild) carp, fish without enough food to go round. None was larger than 5lb or so. From another deep carp pool some miles away I brought some 3lb fish, real 'jumpers', and when I next visited the pond a couple of summers later I found them still jumping merrily. Fish leaping in a pool add greatly to its interest and there is no other coarse fish which is so active or shows itself so much in still water as a jumping carp. (We call the small ones 'splatters', for they seem to rattle the water.)

From observing carp in my garden pool at home I have come to the conclusion that this jumping is no more than a healthy skipping and can be likened to the skipping of lambs. It certainly denotes healthy stock. A carp about to jump may be seen to shoot suddenly forward on its side showing a gleam of bronze.

You may sometimes see the dull gold heliograph of a tench when you are out in the punt. Under you the water seems dark and of a deep olive colour and all at once there comes a secret golden gleam as a tench turns momentarily on its side and the light is reflected on its scales.

The tench never jump, as far as I can see, at least not in the Wood Pool. Sometimes after a prolonged spell of hot weather they will do a porpoise roll on the surface but they never come clean out.

These admirable coarse fish have done extremely well in the pool and I usually catch them round about the same spot:

the three thick islands of bulrush which grow in the shingly neck of the pool close to the island. It is a strange thing that tench are often found in the vicinity of bulrush beds. The bulrush has not the dark-brown fuzzy top (this is reed mace), it is that long dark-green tubular reed which delights in any channel of a river where the current is moving, and which bows over, slowly wagging as mysterious hidden forces move its base.

In the spawning season in late May or early June, if you sit quietly in the boat between these reed islands you may often see the tench moving about among the thick bundles of submerged rod-like roots. Occasionally the tall stems are violently agitated as a big carp pushes its way through them. This fish may be desirous of basking in the very centre of the reed bed where it feels secure from the attention of herons, or it may be a male in pursuit of a gravid female.

I do not think the carp actually lay their eggs in the bulrush islands, they prefer the thicker, shorter sedge close by on the northern edge of the pool.

On a still, hot morning of early summer if I steal up quietly in the boat from under cover of the island lime trees, loud splashings and plungings can be heard from among the thick sedges. By a cautious approach and by thrusting the prow gently into the herbage, the big carp can be seen in the throes of mating.

Sometimes a hen fish will shoulder its way out of the sedge bed and charge across the pool with her attendant in full pursuit. This usually ends in a threshing and splashing in mid water, either fish leaping out and falling back with a bang which rocks the pond. Sometimes if I am watching one of the double-figure fish at close quarters it will suddenly become suspicious. If really scared it will make a panic bolt and dive, but if not quite so sure it will slowly submerge like a submarine. Gradually the blue smoky shape becomes more dim as it sinks slowly out of sight. Then, when well down, a foot or more, the fish often rushes off; you can tell this by the uneasy motion on the surface of the water.

CHAPTER FOUR

The Island Battle

The island is not quite halfway down the lake, it is nearer the western end. In length it is no more than 35 yards, its width is barely 20.

A dozen or more trees grow on it: limes and birches and a black poplar. The largest is the poplar which has an enormous trunk full of crannies and cracks and with slabs of loose bark; a favourite nesting site for tree creepers.

There is a lime or two whose branches hang low over the water and whose sweet golden flowers are loud with bees in the summer heats. The rest are birches, which with age are beginning to swoon outwards into the pool. Some have already done this and those sunken snags are not helpful if one should hook a big fish. These trees were evidently planted by the old squire with an eye to their reflected beauty, and in winter they do indeed make a pretty picture with their silvery stems.

There are a few hawthorn bushes on the island and the remains of an old wire pen where the mallard used to be reared. Few mallard can hatch there now, though I find a nest each year among the brambles inside the pen. The place is infested with rats and their holes are all over the island. On the south side, where the bright-green soft leaves of the lime hang, there is a favourite place for basking carp. The big fish like to swim there, they prefer it to any other part of the pond. You will always find carp prefer cruising under overhanging branches, and they must pick up numberless grubs and caterpillars which fall off the leaves. Even a sunken tree which has bare branches attracts them on hot days and their bluish forms may be seen idling among the snags. Of course they are impregnable in such a place. If you hook one on a floating bait you are snagged in a moment.

One of the reasons why the carp prefer that side of the pond is because the sun shines all day upon the water and the island acts as a wind-break. I have known days when the main pool was ruffled like a rug and the water by the island was as still as a mirror.

The whole surface of the island is covered with ground ivy which makes quite a pleasant couch. When landing on it I do so with as little noise as possible. I pole up through the reed channel and 'finish with engines' some distance off, steering the Swedish boat in under the hanging birches until the prow bumps the matted shelf of tree roots.

I tie up to a hawthorn and step ashore. This, the north side of the island, never gets the sun and on the hottest day it is cool and dark.

Quietly I advance through the stinging nettles and ivy to the opposite side. The sun makes bright coins of light among the leaves, and the water out in front is amber gold, dotted with the white flowerets of water daisy. These make a drift of dusty white over the surface of the pool at the height of the flowering season in June. A few marked spikes stick up from the water against the warm amber glare, branches of sunken birches too large to pull out. There in the cool olive-green shadows the beetles weave and circle and the crane flies dance; truly a pleasant place to be and one of the best pitches for fishing floating bread.

It was from the island that a friend called David and I had our first big thrill and this important occasion must be set on record.

The reader may not remember now, but the June of 1957 was a particularly lovely month, more like the summers we remembered when we were boys.

David arrived on the evening of the fourteenth. He brought with him an impressive Mark IV carp rod and fixed-spool reel. His tackle put me to shame as I never take enough care of my gear and have lost good fish in consequence. My outfit consisted also of a 10-foot Mark IV carp rod built for me by Richard Walker of Hitchin, who is certainly the equal of any of the old-time anglers in skill and knowledge, a worthy successor to Sheringham.

I cannot get along with fixed-spool reels. For one who pretends to be a fisherman this may seem a curious statement. To tell the truth, I have never mastered the art of handling one of these modern reels. In expert hands they are superb; one can cast a tremendous distance which is important when carp fishing in some waters. I rely on a centre-pin duralumin reel which was also made for me by Richard Walker. This has a 4 inch diameter drum which gives terrific recovery and it is far less heavy than the old wooden reels. I think it is as light as bakelite, or other modern plastics.

We reached the boat-house around 5 a.m., our waders wet to the tops with dew. There was that grey, hushed look about the dawn, when the cries of birds are sharpened, when all the woods are murmuring with the cooings of the wood pigeons, and the sharp points to the firs seem alert and listening.

I undid the padlocks on the boat-house door. We clumped inside, smelling the tarred aroma of the interior of the old shed. As we walked across the wooden staging a swallow fled from its nest in the corner *weekaweeking* in alarm, and a wren whirred from another corner where its leaf house was tucked in an angle of the woodwork.

Tackle was packed aboard and checked (nothing is more annoying than arriving at your chosen pitch, after perhaps a long row, to find you have left the landing net behind; it has happened to me before now).

We set off down Congo Channel, disturbing a mallard duck which fled quacking loudly into the reed forests. Sedge warblers scolded and somewhere a cuckoo was calling.

The day, though dull now, promised to be hot. There was a mist about, "pride of the morning," said David, packing his pipe, "the carp should be feeding at sun up."

We emerged from the opening in the reeds where Congo Channel joins the main pool and a party of at least twenty mallard rose in a quacking crowd from beside the island. They swung around us once or twice and made away. I had now stopped paddling. The boat glided softly on to bump gently on the peaty bank under the hanging leaves. I stepped ashore as quietly as I could, for vibration can be felt by sensitive fish.

David went to the east side of the island where there is a

leaning silver birch. This was a good pitch. Forty yards away was a big clump of true bulrush, a favourite 'rolling' ground for the 'double duty' carp.

I picked a slightly less favourable pitch looking west from the side of the island. I say 'less favourable' because there are one or two fallen birches along this side and struck carp will often run along parallel to the bank for the sanctuary of these snags. There is also a hanging branch of lime which makes casting tricky. I could have this bough off but it would ruin the vista and in any case the fish like to cruise about in its green shade on the chance of picking up a fallen grub or caterpillar from the leaves above.

David was fishing without a float, of course, for those who like to try their strength with the big chaps dispense with such boyish adornments. But, let me confess it, I dislike fishing without a float; watching a ledger line is the least exciting form of fishing there is, even when you have a silver paper 'tell tale' on the line.

On my reel I had 100 yards of 8lb B.S. nylon and a No. 2 Model Perfect hook, one small shot to cock my white cork and quill float. I was fishing a big lob in 3 feet of water and at about 30 yards out, just under the outermost sprays of the hanging lime branch.

It was a tricky cast but one I have often done before. I coiled the line from the reel on to my folded coat, and the heavy lob I was using, coupled with the single shot on the line, made it travel out comfortably.

My float was soon riding the water, alert and expectant, just clear of the olive-green shadow. I looked back through the leaves at David. He was sitting hunched on his basket looking out over the pool; clouds of blue 'St Bruno' smoke came puffing round the back of his head from his pipe. There hadn't been much moving up to now. A few small carp ('splatters') were active along the far reed-bed edge, no big chaps as yet, but the sun was not yet over the horizon. That's the time the big fellows wake up for their breakfast.

I threw in six or seven lobs around my float and also a few bits of flake. The bread attracts the small fish and I often think that the big ones come to investigate when they sense 'the children' are getting excited about something.

Now followed one of those quiet contemplative spells where very little happens. Yet never a moment passed without incident. Moorhen larked among the reeds, splashing and *cruiking*, and coots, always the most quarrelsome creatures, chased each other down the far end of the lake in feathers of spray. Then a heron came sailing over. It was amusing to see this excessively wary bird weaving around like a suspicious bombing plane, its circular staring eye searching the scene below. We were well hidden under the island trees and from his wide orbiting he could not possibly have seen us.

When I first stocked the lake the herons soon passed the word around!

I put up a notice board to discourage poachers - No Fishing Allowed. This I planted firmly in the deep water 30 yards from shore, out of reach of mischievous boys. The only access to it was when the pool was locked in ice. This notice board certainly discouraged human poachers but the herons found it a useful digesting perch.

I remember one afternoon when I was walking round with my dogs, I came up the bank and peeped over and there was a heron so gorged he could hardly perch, standing on top of the board! I was sorely tempted to shoot him but my better instincts prevailed, for herons are delightful people and though they may take enormous quantities of fry they also eat eels which are a nuisance in a carp water.

This old fellow circling the pool had evidently made up his mind that everything was nice and quiet. He called a loud *Frank! Frank!* and set his cupped wings. His legs came swaying down and just as he was skimming and rocking over the reeds he caught sight of the white-painted boat under the lime branches. He was so alarmed he let out a jet of 'whitewash' and soared upwards over the trees.

Next, a blunt-nosed vole went arrowing out from the bank. The poor mallard have little chance of rearing their ducklings on this island.

The hands of my watch crept round to seven thirty. Neither David nor I had had a touch though once a very big fish in the 15lb class jumped 50 yards from my float. I saw its broad smooth chestnut side (it was a mirror) rear up and fall back and the ripples came wheeling under the willows breaking up the reflections.

"That was a good'un," called David. I was on the point of pulling in and changing my lob when I thought I noticed a little spinning dimple in the water 10 yards to the right of me where a willow branch comes down at an angle into the water. There was some water buttercup there and this was agitated violently. I knew at once it was one of the big carp. Just as the sun begins to shine on the water the giants often browse among the weed and you can stalk them if there is cover. But it is amazing how sharp their eyesight is. I sat quite still. The miniature whirlpools were creeping nearer along the bank, close in, within a foot of the peaty shelving slope of the island. They formed suddenly, little circular pits like ant bear traps which rotated sideways gradually filling up and becoming shallower and shallower. Somewhere below a broad tail was causing this disturbance.

The sun was now beginning to send shafts of light through the openings in the hanging curtain of leaves and these shafts penetrated the water, shining dimly on the bottom of the pond.

As I watched, a burly mail-clad form appeared, moving very very slowly, rather like a liner creeping into a berth at the dockside.

There were white balls of ground-bait shining dimly where they lay among the fine twigs and leaves. I could see them clearly; they were close to my hook bait. The great fish - he must have been in the fifteen pounder category - was examining this with the utmost caution; it was a lesson for all carp anglers.

His bulging pug-like eyes with their somewhat alarmed expression were fixed on the tempting morsels but he was taking his time about it. Then with an almost imperceptible movement of his tail he began to circle the ground-bait. For a second or so the little white balls were masked as the fully-scaled body (it was a common carp) passed with infinite majesty in front. He swam round five times, this took about three minutes. He then brought up and slowly tilted his head, like an airship being pulled down by the nose. One ball of paste shot upwards by suction. Immediately he had it well in his mouth, he turned and with one terrific sweep of his tail shot out into the lake leaving a spinning whorl of water which passed along in front of me from left to right.

I was so excited at witnessing this incident that my heart was beating fast. At no time could he have been more than a few yards from my hook bait. I was sure he'd come back but there was no sign. I thought of changing over to paste. Then I heard a muffled commotion from the other side of the island and the sound of the check on a reel. It was David, fast into a smallish carp, a mirror of about 6lb. It gave him a lively time before he brought it to the net; these small mirrors fight like tigers sometimes.

This was encouraging. The carp were obviously on the feed though I had an uneasy feeling that zero hour, half-past seven, was well past and I knew that by 9 a.m. all chances of a big carp would be passed.

It was now about three minutes past eight, still time for a run. The sun was quite hot even at this hour and flies were shuttling under the drooping willow leaves. But there, out in the ochre sun-warmed water the white quill lay becalmed.

I was just on the point of going across to see if David had had any more runs when I thought I detected a tremble of the float. It gave one tiny bob. Perhaps a small carpling was sucking at the tail of the lob. Then before I knew what was happening, it was slowly moving away, submerging as it went.

I was sure it was a small fish, it might even be a tench, for they will tackle a lob twice as long as themselves. But as the quill moved off purposefully, submerging as it did so, it gathered speed. By this time I had gripped the cork butt, the coiled line was almost out. I struck from the reel and knew at once this was no tench or carpling, it was one of the big boys. He went straight out into the middle of the lake with a most impressive rush. Had I checked him it would have meant disaster. He went straight for the big bulrush beds. He was still travelling when I brought the check on the reel. (This is a lever which can be moved with the two hind fingers of the right hand.)

I didn't want my adversary to gain the shelter of the tough reeds. I knew he'd go right into them, for they have open pools in the centre, and I got a side pressure to bear, the rod bowed over. David had heard the reel singing and he now came across: "You've got one there, 'BB'."

I was too excited to reply. I managed to turn my fish just before he reached the sanctuary and then he made a great sweep right-handed, travelling across our front and going at such a pace that a feather of spray sprouted from the cutting line.

To the right of the island at the entrance to Frog Channel (see map, page 13) there was a dense bed of water daisy. The swans do not feed up this channel and the growth grows unchecked unless I attend to it with the cutters.

The fish went straight into this with a considerable bow wave which slopped among the reeds. He seemed immovable. I tried hand-lining but dared not put on too much strain. David then went across the island to get the boat and bring it round. It is always wise to have a boat handy in cases like this, as many a big carp is lost if you cannot approach in the boat and free the line, though this has to be done with the utmost caution.

Whilst David was rowing round, the carp suddenly decided to come out of his own accord. He went off at a fast pace for the opposite reeds, still taking line. I shouted to David to finish with engines because I didn't want the fish to go under the boat.

There now developed a ding-dong battle of pully-hauly, with the fish still taking line in fierce rushes. But he kept opposite us in the open water and was soon going in circles deep down. Up to now I hadn't seen the carp but I knew it was a walloper by the power of his pull. A few minutes later he broke surface for the first time with a mighty plunge and we saw he was a massive common carp, possibly the one I had seen earlier inspecting the bait.

David brought the boat quietly along the bank under the trees and had the net ready as the carp came past. The next moment it was thumping a broad tail on the bank. It weighed 14lb 10oz on the spring-balance. We returned it on the far side of the island. I never like putting a fish back at the spot where you catch it.

This specimen was in splendid condition and had been hooked in the ideal spot, at the corner of the mouth.

We had made so much commotion in landing it that it was useless to fish on any longer. Apart from that, it was nearly nine o'clock and we were ready for breakfast.

So much for the first sizeable fish from the lake. The warm June weather continued, false promise of a hot summer which unfortunately failed to materialise.

David had struck lucky coming when he did. Each day was fine and warm with little wind, ideal fishing weather. Though we tried the island pool on the three mornings after, for we judged that to be the best bet for a big fish, we never got into another and only three and four pounders rewarded our efforts.

For the evenings I decided to move down to the channel between the reed islands. I'd seen some of the big chaps on the move there early and late. Curiously enough a few very large ones were jumping right against the reeds on the west bank in about 3 feet of water. I think carp like to 'jolly' along the sides of the reeds. They coast from bay to bay and pick up all kinds of trifles which have fallen from the vegetation.

It wasn't until David's last evening that we got into another of the patriarchs. This proved the most exciting battle of them all.

The day had been excessively hot and we did not begin operations until half-past eight, and even that was far too early. But I wanted to get some ground-bait down and give the fish time to find it.

It meant also fishing from the boat which I intended to moor between the reed islands. I was not too sanguine about this as when you are after the big fellows you should be under cover on dry land.

There was no other way of reaching the deep channel and it was a favourite swim for fish passing through the neck of the lake to the upper reaches. This channel was originally the old bed of the brook which once wandered down the meadows.

It was a close, overcast evening and nothing big appeared to be moving, only a few 'splatters' busy in the reed beds and along the margins close to the rushes.

Almost as soon as we started to fish we were plagued with small tench which kept pulling the tails of the lobs and running about with the end of the worm in their mouths. Then they ceased to worry and, like Sheringham, we 'took heart of grace' for this might well mean the big boys were coming up. It began to get dusky around 10 p.m. and I had a feeling that something was going to happen. I had that strange presentiment of impending events carpfishers often get.

A little after ten had struck from the distant church tower in the village (the strokes plainly heard in the quiet atmosphere) my quill slipped away without fuss. I thought it was another of the plaguing tench but I was soon disillusioned.

The carp ran down the centre of the lake when I hit him; there was no holding him. He then came back straight for the boat. I thought I'd lost him, but with the big calibre centre-pin I just about kept pace with him.

He then made a very determined run towards the dam and at that moment the mooring reeds parted from the rowlocks. (I must explain that I had moored the boat simply by twisting a bunch of bulrush stems round the rowlocks, a habit I have when boatfishing.)

The result was both dramatic and amusing for as soon as the boat broke free the fish took us at a steady pace down his initial track, straight for the centre of the lake, it was as if we had the outboard motor on the back!

There was a lot of bad language then for it went straight into the water plantain by the dam. I had meant to deal with this weed the week before just prior to the opening of the season, but I had never got round to doing it, principally because I had planted some white water lilies there and they were just showing among the plantains. Now I had my deserts.

That carp weeded us good and hard. We brought the boat right over him and for a time I could feel an occasional response on the line but we couldn't do much. Then a strange mishap occurred. The carp must have suddenly decided to forsake the cover of the plantains and somehow got the line free on his own accord. But at that moment I had turned away and was giving useless advice to David who was probing gently with the handle of the net.

My rod was resting on the gunwale of the boat on the port side. The big fish shot down almost vertically and in an instant the top joint of my rod had gone at the ferrule; it was goodbye to the carp, float, and all!

What that fish weighed I have no idea. We never even saw it. But it must have been one of the very big ones.

Definitely one up to the carp!

CHAPTER FIVE

Night Fishing

As a general rule it might be said that if you want a 'glass case' carp you should fish at night.

This is absolutely essential in a carp water which is very much fished. The average angler dislikes night fishing and for some reason or another many angling clubs would like to see it banned altogether.

There is not the slightest doubt that the very big ones feed best in the darkness. Richard Walker caught the record forty-four pounder in Redmire in the small hours of an intensely black September night, so black he could not see his hand before his face.

It is true that occasionally a big fish may be taken on floating bread during the noonday heats and on a water which is seldom fished. Where the carp have been educated to floating bread this form of fishing sometimes pays off.

Fishing with floating bread is most exciting and calls for

considerable skill. A water I know well and used to fish in Lincolnshire held some very big mirrors around the 20lb mark. This pond was fished assiduously by charabanc parties and angling clubs during the hours of daylight but never a carp was caught. As is usual in such places, enough ground-bait was hurled in to feed a regiment but it was ignored until the last charabanc had departed and had 'left the pool to darkness and to them'. Even so the fish did not begin to feed until nearly midnight. But feed they did, and in company with that master carper, Maurice Ingham of Louth, I had some runs and a fish or two around the 10lb class; the best for that water is I believe 18lb.

This was a clear case of a much-fished water which yielded really big specimens if tackled in the right way. Fish, like most other creatures, form habits. For years these big carp had lain doggo during the daytime when the banks were lined with anglers and had ventured forth only when all was dark and quiet.

The truth of the matter is that night fishing calls for considerable fortitude on the part of the angler. He must keep on the alert and if fishing alone, must be impervious to 'ghoulies and ghosties'. Many carp waters are mysterious, tree-girt places, often of immense depth such as at Redmire, which I have often fished.

Though the species is wily, it can be easily tamed, as can be seen by the continental carp such as those at Versailles, and in moats and ponds of many a German Schloss.

Perhaps continual ground-baiting may seem a little unfair and savour of the unsporting, like feeding hand-reared pheasants and then shooting them. In most ponds where the carp are regarded as impregnable the visiting angler has no time to tame them. If he is lucky he may have three or four days at the most. He must fish at night and take his chances.

In the late summer of 1957 a Northampton angler landed two carp in one night, both in the 30lb class, and this was from a well-fished carp pit near the town. He began to fish when others had gone home and caught them both after extensive ground-baiting carried on for a number of days.

Strange as it may seem, the most difficult place to try for big carp is that type of parkland pool which is seldom, if ever, fished. The fish are quite uneducated to bread. They may take a lob worm, but even where they have been unmolested for years their natural sagacity is still evident, and unless some ground-baiting is done a few days before it will be a very lucky man who gets into a worthwhile specimen.

In the Wood Pool where the carp have only recently been introduced they certainly bite much more freely. I suppose I do not fish it more than a dozen times during the season and it is a strictly private water. Few big chaps have had the experience of being hooked and lost, save the odd ones which have broken me and my friends. I am sure that where big carp are much fished for and have been scared on a number of occasions they are all the more wary; like the elephant, they never forget.

A great number of words have been written lately about when and why carp feed. Walker, who is of a practical and scientific turn of mind, takes the temperature of the water when he fishes. His findings are all set down in his own excellent books on the subject, *Still Water Angling* and *Drop Me a Line.*

I don't intend to pick the many juicy morsels of information which he offers in both these books; the reader must find them for himself, unless he has already done so. Nor do I intend this little book to be a treatise on 'how to catch carp'. In any case I do not consider myself a skilled angler, but I do boast that I am a good observer and naturalist; even if one is a bad and slovenly fisherman (which I am) this does help a great deal when after glass-case specimens.

Up to a few years ago, let us say fifteen or twenty years, carp were quite neglected as a sporting fish. It is true there were, up and down the country, a few solitary carp catchers who had a weakness for them. Names such as Overbeck and Buckley and of course Sheringham, though he was not a genuine carp catcher. Men such as these had some good fish in their time but nobody guessed that the species went over 26lb. Indeed, in *Fishes of The British Isles,* Travis Jenkins quotes Tate Regan as saying the limit in Britain was 25lb. (This from the second edition in 1926.)

It is a puzzle why no carp larger than this had been caught prior to Buckley's at Mapperley in 1930. Perhaps it was because big carp had a reputation for being quite uncatchable, and had produced a sort of inferiority complex amongst anglers. When on rare occasions one was hooked by accident it was regarded as a misfortune, for it was 'good-bye' to your tackle.

In the nineteen-thirties I was busy compiling my *Fisherman's Bedside Book* and during the process I was quite intrigued by the reports of Buckley's twenty-six pounder from Mapperley. I contacted him and got him to write me an account of what actually happened, and this went into the book.

His story stirred something in another angler's mind. That Christmas, Richard Walker had my book given him and I had an enthusiastic letter from him. Thus began a friendship which was to bear much fruit in the future. He brought his scientific mind to bear on the subject, and, in 1951, on the shores of the historic Mapperley reservoir in Derbyshire, the scene of Buckley's capture, he and I, Maurice Ingham, and John Norman, alas, now dead, formed the Carp Catchers' Club which has since accounted for most of the notable specimens caught since 1951.

The members, which now number twelve, exchange correspondence throughout the year, everyone pooling his experience and knowledge. This, you may say, has little to do with the subject of this book, but I mention it because I think it may be useful to know how the interest in carp catching was first aroused. I like to think that Walker and myself have been the pioneers of this branch of angling and have explored hitherto unknown fields, or shall I say 'waters'. Much might be done by other specialists with tench and barbel and certainly with perch. I am sure that there are waters in Britain which hold far larger tench than the present record of 8lb 8oz and the same applies to perch.

Both Walker and Ingham use buzzers for night fishing. This again was one of Walker's inventions and I see that similar gadgets can now be bought ready-made. They consist of an ordinary torch battery housed in a case; the line is clipped in to a trigger mechanism. When the fish takes the ledger line it pulls it from between two contacts, which immediately connect and the alarm sounds. In the more elaborate designs a light flashes on.

I have used these things with some success but had to give them up for a peculiar reason.

In night fishing, alone, and towards the early hours, sleep is often so overpowering that one must take a few 'cat naps' to be at the alert when necessary.

On a number of occasions when I have been feeling absolutely ill for sleep I have dropped off. Invariably the alarm has gone off and the shock has been something which I personally find very bad for me. This may sound laughable but one must remember that for hours at a time one's senses have been keyed up expecting a run. When I attach the line I am waiting for the buzz. If it comes when I am in a deep sleep it is for me, at least, as great a shock as if I had been plunged into icy water without warning.

The old dodge of silver paper clipped on the reel line is as good as any, if you are awake. I am not sure what penalties should be inflicted on the sleeping carp catcher; perhaps they should be as severe as those for a sentry caught sleeping at his post!

I would say that the zero hour for the leviathans is around 4 and 5 a.m. during the carping season.

At Redmire I have often fished all night alone and a very eerie experience it was.

Redmire is an immensely deep water girt with trees. On one side there is a great cleft down which runs a little stream. When I was last there I was camping in a tent close to the pool and I knew that somewhere in the meadows below the dam an ill-tempered bull was at large. During the hours of darkness I heard this old gentleman moving about along the banks of the stream, blowing and crackling among the underwood. It wasn't a happy vigil and I had no bites. Indeed, though I am President of the Carp Catchers' Club, I have yet to land a carp from Redmire! I must be one of the few members who have not done so. Perhaps it is a measure of my skill, or the lack of it.

I often think that had I connected with one of the truly unbelievable fish in the pool (I have seen a carp far larger than the record forty-four pounder) I should have been quite powerless to land it unaided. It is doubtful if Walker would ever have brought his fish to bank without the aid of Pete Thomas. (This specimen at the time of writing is still alive and well in the Aquarium at the London Zoo, magnificent proof that anglers do not always lie.)

The nearest I ever came to catching one of these stupendous fish was one late June evening when I was fishing from the shallow eastern end. It was an ideal evening with sun after rain. Delicious scents were perfuming the air, scents of lush-growing plants, grass, leaves, wild mint, and reeds, all wet and warm, the kind of scents one notices in a greenhouse, but more rare and subtle, and which only belong to June.

I had seen a very broad back and pair of shoulders moving stealthily among weed about 50 yards from the bank. I reached the spot with a long cast and settled down to wait. The bait at Redmire is bread paste. (One can use worms but the place is infested with eels and they take them at once.)

I had been fishing for about an hour with a ball of paste the size of a bantam's egg, in about 4 feet of water much weeded up. A small boy from the nearby farm came down to see what I was doing. Just as he came charging down the bank on a bicycle my bait was taken. Unfortunately at that very moment I had turned to tell him to keep quiet. When I looked round the fish had ripped off 20 yards of line and just as I picked up the butt it left with the bait.

It was shocking bad luck. I have fished there for many hours; once I went for three days and never had a bite. I have never had another opportunity. As Redmire is some way from my home I have had to take a chance on the weather. So far it has always been shockingly bad, cold and wet, all save that one warm night when the boy spoilt my chance. But that's the luck of fishing.

As I have said earlier I prefer fishing with a float though I doubt whether many of the very big 'glass-case' specimens have been caught on anything but leadless tackle. A float just adds that extra amount of excitement for me. On the other hand, this may be one of the reasons for my unsuccess at Redmire.

At Redmire there is always the consoling thought that you may be suddenly taken by a really fabulous fish. I have seen at least one there which was like a bronze row boat. I hesitate to estimate its weight, but I certainly put it at over 50lb.

These creatures seemed to me, in the hours of darkness, as fish not of this earth. They are at least prehistoric monsters.

Those who have fished at night for sea trout will understand the eerie atmosphere of a river. Yet the constant sound of running water and the splash of jumping trout are cheerful sounds to the lone angler. Fishing alone at Redmire in the blackness of a summer night it is as silent as a vault. Big carp seldom jump during the hours of darkness, and there is no companionable sound of running water. But there is always the knowledge that some fantastic fish may be looming through those hidden deeps and drawing to the bait as stealthily as a tiger to its kill.

Unfortunately certain changes have come to Redmire, notably the introduction of numerous ducks which are a perfect nuisance, diving for the bread at night and sometimes even trying to hook themselves.

Also, a recent warm summer, which proved ideal for the breeding carp, produced thousands of fry. These are just coming to the age of being a nuisance. Still, I hope to get my monster yet.

CHAPTER SIX

Congo Channel

When I first came to my present home Wood Pool was rapidly going dry and becoming grown up with weeds. It was quite impossible to find one's way out to the open lake through the sedges and reeds, for the shallower water had grown up solid. There was little to be done save to have it cleaned out professionally which is a horribly costly job, entailing traction engines, cranes, and heaven knows what else. A thousand pounds might cover the cost, but only just.

All I could do was to mend the leaks and cut a narrow channel out from Boat-House Pond to the open water, a matter of 600 yards distance. When I got down to the job, having repaired the boat, I found traces through the reeds where once a channel had been. This was obviously the old stream bed. A glance at the map may help the reader.

It will be seen that the small railed-in spring above Boat-House Pond is the only source of supply and that by the boat-house itself is the original pond, no more than a horse pond. From it the water flowed away through the reed jungles to the open lake.

I took down a long-handled small scythe and a rake. Donning thigh boots I found that once I was clear of the old pond which was about 6 feet deep, I could wade for many yards with the water only an inch or so below the tops of my waders. The bottom was quite firm, indeed most of the lake-bottom is gravel.

It was hard work. Some of the sedges I could pull up by the roots, but when I came upon a clump of true bulrush it defeated me. I doubt whether anything but a steam tractor can clean this obnoxious rush out of a pond.

By degrees I cleared a winding channel, following the track of the old stream all the time until I came to where the lake deepened and it was impossible to wade any farther. I then had to get aboard the boat and work as best as I could from that, but the job I did was not so thorough. By dint of perseverance I managed at last to reach the open water of the lake just west of the tail of the island. There I cleared another strip - Frog Channel - which leads to the right of the island and serves as a short-cut home to the boat-house, though I seldom use it.

After progressing some hundred yards from the boat-house down my new channel, which I named Congo Channel, I came to open pools among the reed mace. These were favourite haunts for mallard at all hours of the day.

When the fish became established it was also a favourite basking and grubbing place for carp and tench. The carp especially seemed to favour it, coming up from the main lake on warm summer evenings when all was quiet.

Here too the cattle came to drink. This may have been an

added attraction to the carp, for where the cattle 'stomp' the bottom of a pond they attract feeding fish.

Among these reed mace beds, in the shallow pools, it was delightful to watch some of the bigger fish cruising quietly about. The water was crystal clear, as it often is near bulrush beds, and the big chaps could be seen gliding from pool to pool each with a shadow beneath it.

There in the spring of the year the great golden goblets of the king cups bloom and the air is fragrant with water mint.

As one paddles up Congo Channel from the boat-house it is easy to imagine one is in some tropical swamp and that round the next bend one may catch sight of a sleeping crocodile, or surprise a buffalo drinking.

The reeds in high summer are well above one's head and you can only see the winding path of water, the tall waving reeds, and the vivid blue summer sky overhead.

Being without shade (reeds give negligible shade) the sun beats down, or seems to do so, with tropical ferocity. As you pole along the mud has an evil smell, for it is deep here at the head of the lake.

So complete is this illusion of a tropical swamp I cannot bring myself to imagine that this wilderness of reed and water was ever an open marshy meadow. But such it was, less than half a century ago. So man can, by the work of his hands and the sweat of his temples, alter and transform a landscape.

I have lately seen an old faded photograph, yellow with age, in an album at the 'big house'. It shows gangs of labourers in little round, almost peakless, caps busy with planks and barrows excavating this very lake. It dates perhaps somewhere about the year I entered into the scheme of things - about 1905 perhaps.

This reedy wilderness was once open meadow, starred with buttercups and 'milkmaids', and now it is this tropical swamp full of exciting things!

One afternoon of great heat, when I was poling back along Congo Channel, I saw in front of me a furl of water cleaving the winding silver stream. As the prow of the boat drew silently and softly nearer I stood up in the thwarts and saw before me, swimming along with a rowing motion of its 'arms', a water tortoise. How it came to be there I shall never know, nor where it went to, for after the boat glided almost on his shell for 10 to 15 yards it vanished under the keel and I saw it no more. How that creature completed for me the illusion of the tropical swamp!

There have been other days of heat when I have seen snakes swimming down the channel ahead of my boat, harmless lovely grass snakes who rejoice to feel the cool caress of water on their dry, hot flanks. Can you wonder I call this Congo Channel? It was just at the end of it where it widens into the lake by Frog Channel that I found the carcase of a great trout, last survivor of those which lived in the lake after it was stocked by the old squire. It had no mark on it; it had not lain there long, neither the rats nor the crows had touched it. Alive and in its prime it must have weighed 6lb perhaps, a Loch Leven trout with a small head and beautifully proportioned. What had killed it?

There are ironstone workings nearby where blasting is sometimes done. Rumours were current at one time that a poacher had dynamited the pool. Perhaps this was one of the victims, or it may have died of old age. There is still a great deal of doubt about exactly how long fish may live. Tate Regan, who was perhaps the greatest authority on these matters, had the opinion that the age of fish is exaggerated and that carp do not live to be hundreds of years old as was popularly believed.

The bed of the pool close to the bulrush beds is hard gravel and on very hot days I pole up Congo Channel and moor the boat between the reed islands. The effort of pushing up from the boat-house shade is almost unbearable. There is a short respite as I glide in the lee of the island, for the cool shadow rests the eyes. There, too, the small black flies shuttle to and fro just over the surface, and maybe a swirl in front of the gliding prow shows where a carp has gone down.

I am soon out again into the burning rays and what a relief it is to strip off my coat and trousers and dive, otter-like, over the prow of the boat! The green-lit water is tolerably clear and there are no weeds to hamper me if I keep to the open pools. Lazily I swim around, just moving arms and legs sufficiently to keep me waterborne. A sudden arrowing swirl shows where a big fish has taken fright, blue dragonflies flit overhead, the dark purple patches on the tips of their wings fascinating to watch.

Everywhere is the sense of high summer. In the gaps between the hawthorns on the north bank the buttercup fields are ablaze with varnished gold, the cuckoos call lazily away in the woods behind, the sedge warblers *zitt, zitt, churr, churr,* close at hand, turtle doves croon from the willows.

Then I swim back to the boat, hauling myself over the stern, feeling the hot painted boards under cool toes. Then one can lie in the bottom of the boat and watch the shadowed depths beside the reed bed. It will not be long before there is a movement and I glimpse perhaps a shoal of carp, head to tail, passing gently under the keel. Or more exciting still, the slow-gliding grandfather who materialises like a cloud and seems to melt away again, all so gently that I wonder if I have imagined it.

On hot days every opening in the water-daisy weeds provides a basking place for the numerous (alas! too numerous) baby tench. They cluster into the sun-warmed spots and are very difficult to see, even when you bring the boat almost alongside the openings. Suddenly they dive like miniature seals and the *plop plop* of startled tenchlings resounds on all sides.

Big carp also delight in these small openings and if I cruise quietly along I can see the familiar bluish humped back rise and fall among the weeds. They lie for half-an-hour or more almost motionless, letting the sun warm their bulky shining bodies.

CHAPTER SEVEN

Hints on Carp Tackle

I've no business to be writing this chapter because I have never professed to be an expert angler. There are plenty of books, and very good ones too, on how to catch carp and tench. Nevertheless this has to be written, for it may well be that the reader has been fired with a desire to catch a big carp and may think I have not been very precise in my description of suitable tackle.

I get into the most dreadful trouble with my fellow members of the Carp Catchers' Club whenever I fish in their company. My rods are examined minutely with many shakings of the head, and the state of my reels and lines cause sundry clicks of the tongue. You see, the truth is that if you are to be an expert fisherman you must be a very tidy, precise sort of person, who can fiddle with almost invisible flies and casts and keep every particle of tackle in its proper place. This is utterly beyond me. My reels get dirty, even rusty, I am guilty of using the same line season after season and I never, under any circumstances, take the trouble to dry it. So you can see why I do not consider myself a fit person to offer advice to anyone. Yet strange as it may seem, I *have* caught large carp and have played and landed large trout so I am not a complete duffer. Moreover I possess (though I say it myself) a keen eye for likely localities and am blessed with that subtle sixth sense of the sportsman, the sort of sense which tells me the best place to waylay a wily greylag goose on the dawn flight and the most likely lie for a trout in a brook.

Without this sense even the most skillful angler cannot always hope to be successful. It is the combination of the two qualities, good 'watercraft' and attention to tackle which makes for the perfect fisherman. Your country poacher is often more successful in getting a fish (by legitimate means, mark you, in so far as tackle goes) than the visiting angler who has no 'stream craft'.

First then, what is the best rod for big carp? And, after all, it is big carp which concern me in my lake; anyone can catch small fish up to 2lb.

It is wise to remember that you are going to use a fairly stout line, anything upwards of 6lb breaking strain, which I would put as the minimum for dealing with carp in the 15lb category. Your line may well have to be 12lb breaking strain if you are dealing with fish of the Redmire calibre: there you have heavy weed to contend with and hidden snags. Because of this heavy line you need a strong rod which is at the same time nice to handle, with a pleasant spine. And there is, in my opinion, only one rod which fits this description perfectly, and that is the two-piece Mark IV carp rod which is, I believe, now retailed by B. James of Ealing. It is of split cane with agate tip ring, large intermediate rings, and a stand-off butt ring which has a diameter of 26 millimetres. It is in two joints and the overall length is 10 feet with a cork handle 30 inches long.

If you wish to build this rod yourself, and nowadays many anglers are doing so, thereby saving many pounds for their pockets, you can find full details in Richard Walker's own book *Rod Building for Amateurs.* Walker, of course, designed the rod and its younger brother the Mark IV Avon.

With this weapon you can of course spin for salmon or pike and it has the great merit of being able to throw weights of all sizes up to $1^{1}/_{2}$oz comfortably. It can flip a lob on a 6lb line an incredible distance, or even, for that matter, a large ball of paste.

As to lines, it is best, as in salmon fishing, to have all your line in one length, preferably nylon or Perlon. If you are going to try your hand at floating bread for carp then monofilament is best, and it is wise to dye these lines to suit the water in which you intend to fish. In my early days I confess to using banjo strings for dealing with the very big carp. I must say that in weedy water a banjo string cuts through obstructions exceedingly well and has saved me losing many a good fish, but the Perlon monofilament line will serve your purpose best. There is something savouring of the unsporting in using wire for carp. As to hooks, these must be kept sharp and the best is undoubtedly the Model Perfect forged hook in sizes 2, 3, and 4.

Some carp fishers prefer treble hooks, indeed an old postman in Devon, whom I used to meet on many a pearly summer's morn beside the banks of the old Copper Mine, always swore by treble hooks. Again I feel that if you can't catch a big one on a single hook you have no business trying to catch him on a treble. It's akin to shooting wild geese with an 8-bore when a 3 inch magnum 12 will do the job just as well, and much more cleanly.

Your really dyed-in-the-wool carp catcher, such as the members of my own club, will not own a float.

As to reels, the reader may prefer to use his own special brand of fixed-spool reel and there are many on the market, both English and foreign. In the cheaper category, the French C.A.P. reel is an excellent job. I used it for one or two seasons until, through my own clumsiness and lack of skill, I had the line in a mess in the dark over the pick-up and lost a heavy fish. I believe now that all fixed-spool reels which are worth their salt have a hooped pick-up which cannot entangle the line, but even so I shall stick to the gearless Nottingham style reel which was made for me by Richard Walker. It has enormous recovery powers but will not hold as much line as a fixed spool, and, if you are going to try your strength with the leviathans, you need at least 100 yards on the drum.

One must remember when a fish which may possibly weigh 30lb takes hold, he will have a run for his money however hard you hold him.

I see that Walker advocates the Mitchell fixed-spool reel for those who prefer this type, and these reels will take the necessary 100 yards of line with ease.

A word must be said here about landing nets. Again Richard Walker made mine for me. It has 30 inch arms and a mesh bag 3 feet deep. This will take care of any big fish that I am likely to encounter. Most landing nets sold in the shops are far too small for the man who is out for big carp, and many good fish have been lost at the bank through having too small a net.

Finally as to baits. These vary from water to water but in an untried pool the lob worm is a safe banker, but let it not be too large and 'boa' like. I prefer the three-quarter grown lob, culled from a dewy lawn on a summer's night. He is as glistening and shot with as many colours as a crow's wing. I defy any hungry fish, however old and wise, to turn aside without at least one smack of his lips! The only snag is that small fish often grab him first. Bread paste is next best. Some swear that honey should be mixed with it but I believe that this is only an angler's fancy, just as some fishermen tint their paste or maggots appetising colours of custard yellow or shrimp-pink.

If you are after the giants, let your ball of paste be large, at least as big as a bantam's egg. One thing is very certain, the grandfather carp like something to get hold of; apart from that, the tiddlers will leave you alone. It is a strange fact that in all the good carp waters that I have fished up and down the country eels are always present. They take your lob and arouse at first hope and excitement in your breast which turns to revulsion and disappointment. I do not like eels on my hook, they are somehow indecent and obscene, and make me feel I really *am* a fisher for coarse creatures!

An eel in the frying pan is a different matter and I have a great weakness for them. I remember once fishing in company with Dick Walker by a lake in Rutland which was reputed to hold big carp (actually they turned out to be bream), and I had eels every morning for breakfast, whoppers of 2lb or more, many of them caught on night lines.

The skinning of an eel puts many people off, but it is a simple operation. With a sharp knife you make an incision round the neck behind the gills. You then grip the skin edge with a pair of pliers. The skin peels off with a dry rustle like a strip of bark off a willow twig; underneath the flesh is dry and faintly blue, like perch flesh, firm and sweet. They are the nicest eating of all the freshwater fish, bar trout.

Finally, a word or two as to weather conditions, for these are certainly important to the carp catcher. It is useless to expect to catch them in cold weather, and sometimes it is very cold even at the height of the season. At the same time, in the middle of a hot spell, large carp seem lethargic, though this is the most favourable time to use the floating bread method, for they are invariably up on the surface basking and lazily swimming around, usually three or four big fish together; they appear to be sociable creatures.

I have done little good ledgering for big carp *during* a hot spell. The best time of all is during a change of temperature, preferably from cold to warm, and this especially applies to night fishing. Thundery weather is usually regarded as hopeless for most kinds of fish save eels but this certainly does not apply to carp, for many big fish have been captured when thunder is about.

Of course if you do adopt the floating bread method, a centre-pin reel is not suitable. You will be better off with a fixed spool which will enable you to cast a long way out. The golden rule for floating bread fishing is 'fine as you dare and far off', fine because your line must float on the surface after being well dressed with water-resisting substance, and far-off because the big chaps invariably keep to the centre of the pool in daylight hours. I have found Snowfire, a commercial preparation for chilblains, most effective for this job, but the proprietary brands sold for this purpose are more efficient.

For bait, the centre of a new loaf, a fairly large morsel, is best, for it floats for a long time. Just dip it lightly once in the water before you cast and it will take on that added weight necessary to carry it out. Old bread is not so good. Some anglers favour cubes, but these soon become sodden and sink. Remember that before a carp takes a floating bait it invariably inspects it, swimming around and around, often for a considerable time, before making up his mind. When he does grab it, it is usually with a sudden gulp. You should not strike until he has turned and is travelling with it in his mouth.

When bottom fishing, whether you use a float or not is up to you. A float is something to watch. But if you are out for a record breaker I think you should dispense with it and ledger on the bottom, as do all virtuous carp catchers.

In many waters, potatoes are the bait, but the fish must be educated to them. A potato should be about the size of a walnut. It should be lightly boiled so as to render it soft enough for the hook to pull home on the strike. The top skin is peeled off to make it appear appetising like a shelled hard-boiled egg. I have caught large carp on potato and I find that when they do decide to take the bait there are no half-measures. The great merit of potato is that no other fish, not even an eel, will show any interest in it. I remember fishing a lake in Somerset (Lackey's Leap) which contained specimens in the 15lb category. I had left my rod on its rest, with the potato bait well out into the pool, and had gone along the bank to see how Walker was faring. When I returned, the rod was half in the lake and a taut line, 60 yards or more, stretched across the neck of the lake to the far side. I landed this fish of about 8lb. He had hooked himself. It is a risky business leaving rods on their rests. I know a man who, returning along the bank, was just in time to see his rod diving like a javelin into the deeps. He never saw it again!

Carp are nearly omnivorous. They will take many varied baits, maggots, worms, peas and beans. Dick Walker caught a sixteen pounder on a piece of plum cake. They have even been known to take live-bait, but this is most unusual.

In the very early summer mornings the big fish leave the deeps where they have been spending the night and cruise about the shallows, browsing in the weeds like pigs. This is a deadly time if you can manage to stalk them, but they are as wary as chub; if they sense the slightest suspicious movement or vibration they gradually sink from sight. Often they are so intent on feeding that they stick their vast polished backs well out of the water. They make sucking sounds and loud smacks which give the watcher the impression they are thoroughly enjoying their meal, which no doubt they are.

There is no 'best time' for big carp. I prefer the very beginning of the season, early June, or else the beginning of September, just before the winter frosts send them down. Walker caught his forty-four pounder in September and many other large ones have been captured in that month. I suppose it will be some time before this record is beaten, but remember there are bigger fish in Redmire, for I have seen them. One day a fifty pounder will be caught.

Finally a word must be said about carp on the table. For most people the idea of eating one, a mud-loving fish which delights in dirty ponds, is abhorrent, but I can assure them that mirror carp from a gravel-bottomed lake such as the Wood Pool make excellent eating indeed.

Mirrors which are bred in Germany for the table have very few bones, and what bones they have are very easily removed. They need well cooking in a covered pan, or they can be fried in deep fat, or baked in the oven.

Of course a French cook could make any freshwater fish most appetising, even a chub in the hands of a chef might surprise you.

I frequently bring back a brace of 2lb mirrors from the lake and enjoy them for breakfast. The flavour is most delicate and delightful.

Usually if carp dwell in a muddy pond they are beyond the pale, and the common wild carp, which is a much leaner, more rangey fish than the chubby mirrors, are probably poor eating, even out of a clean lake.

Far too few coarse fishermen eat what they catch. I have known men return the most delicious gudgeon to the water, and perch as well; the latter fish out of clear water are even better than mirror carp.

If you intend stocking a water, go to a reputable dealer such as Leney of Haslemere, who will supply both mirror and all-scaled carp. You have only to say which variety you prefer. The mirrors grow more quickly for some reason and it is best to stock up with the larger fry as these are the fast growers. I advise a mixture of all-scaled common carp, mirrors and scale-less or 'leather' carp. The true 'wild' common carp, such as are found in former monastic waters, is a very long lean fish more like a barbel.

If you want fish which will prove stern fighters and attain two-figure weights in a very short period of time, five or six years in a favourable water such as the Wood Pool, then there is no better species than the mirror carp. They are as lively as trout and will gladden the eye and ear by their summer jumping, and will gladden the palate too if the lake is clean.

At one time the carp was an uncommon species, or at least very local in this country, but more and more angling clubs are stocking up with them and this is all to the good.

It is wise to remember however that if you live in the North of England, or in Scotland, it is doubtful if they will do so well as those in the South, for they will lack the warmth and sunlight which is so essential to quick growth and healthy stock.

I understand there are several carp waters in Northumberland but I know of none in Scotland. That may well be because coarse fish in Scotland are not well thought of, understandable in a land where the lordly salmon and princely sea trout hold sway. Perhaps nobody has ever bothered to introduce them there; it may well be worth a trial.

Keep perch out of your pond, and of course pike should be barred. I have known good carp waters which hold both pike and carp but they cover several acres; in small ponds pike are best 'away'.

Carp spawn in May, as soon as the water becomes warm, and at that time, for a week or ten days, the Wood Pool is a lively place. This is the time to see the big ones chasing each other all over the place, leaping and threshing. They make more business of mating than any other coarse fish. Just before spawning, which takes place among the stems of the reeds, carp are lethargic.

Unhappily at this time frogs are also mating and I have often found fish with frogs on their heads. The frogs grip the carp with their thumbs, almost gouging out their eyes, and it takes considerable force to pull the frog away.

Izaak Walton mentions this habit. The explanation is simple. The male frogs, inflamed with sexual desire, will fasten on anything that swims. They must take the carp's head for a female frog.

CHAPTER EIGHT

Habits of Tench

I have perhaps said far too little about my tench in the Wood Pool. This is not because I regard this fish as inferior to the carp; indeed it is a far more attractive species in every way save that the fish tend not to show themselves by jumping and cruising. Many regard the tench as I do, as the most handsome of all the coarse fish. Its lines are Grecian, reminding one of those superb designs in *bas relief* on ancient temples.

The proportions of the tench, fins, head, tail, and girth, are exquisite and well-balanced, and there is something about the round 'deckle edges' to its fins and the thickness of the tail-root which makes its appearance most satisfying.

Tench vary in colour a good deal, from olive-green to a quite golden bronze. This depends on the type of water. Those fish from clean gravel pits are much lighter in colour than tench from deep black ponds where for centuries the trees have shed their leaves into the water.

When I introduced the original fifty 3 inch tenchlings with my stock in 1951 I never thought they would multiply so fast. Abundant pond weed, nearly all of it the meritorious water daisy, no doubt proved ideal for breeding, for this weed gives both food and shelter; food because of the minute insect life it harbours, and shelter, by virtue of its thickness, from marauding herons and kingfishers.

The latter account for an enormous amount of fish fry, as many a trout breeder will tell you. These brilliant birds are abhorred by every trout fishery. In passing I might mention that the manager of the Bibury Trout Farm in Gloucestershire told me that wrens are also a great menace on a hatchery. Apparently they dive as well as kingfishers. Their favourite stance is in some old boat-house, and, now I come to think of it, I have always found wrens in boat-houses, but I have never seen them catching fry.

Kingfishers, like herons, can become bold. During the early winter of the present year, my daughter came running to tell me that there was a 'lovely bird' perched on the willow by my garden pool. This pool, which I made myself, is within 10 yards of my house, and we are a long way from the lake and surrounded by thick woodland.

Sure enough, there was a kingfisher, perched above the pool, and as we watched it dived and came up with a small dace, one of twenty or so which my little boy had caught three years before. We scared the bird away but it returned within twenty minutes. I then hung a piece of metallic paper which kept him away, but after about three weeks he was back again. Finally I had to fire a shot over his head to tell him I meant business for he would have stripped my pond of dace, and I keep these delightful little fish just for the joy of seeing them rising for flies on summer evenings.

But to return to my tench. I have in this same pond about half-a-dozen which I caught myself in a lake near Rugby as far back as 1943. They were fish of over a pound then, so they must be at least eighteen years old. They do not seem to change at all in size, probably due to the lack of water depth and natural food.

Unlike the carp, they are slow growing. A tench of 6lb which is the biggest I have captured, must have been very old indeed. It is a pity we have no real proof of the age of wild fish.

Of course if one is going to fish for a tench you will not need the tackle which you use for a big carp. A 3lb B.S. line should suffice unless the water is full of snags and weeds. The rod can be much lighter. One of the best is the Avon type designed by F. W. K. Wallis which is capable of dealing with big tench if the need arises. As in carp fishing, the rod should be placed in a rest, for 'tenching' is a leisurely business.

In some ways they are curious fish and very temperamental. Sometimes, though, there are tench in a lake that will go 'on strike' and never look at your bait for a year or more and then come on the feed again. Close thundery weather is propitious, and they feed in the same atmospheric conditions as the carp, delighting in warm water, anything over 60° F. They are continually bottom feeders but will occasionally take floating crust, though I have not known this in the lake here.

Worm is the best bait in the Wood Pool, not the very large lob, but the small red 'manure heap' worms. A bunch of these on the hooks is deadly.

I had a surprising experience when tench fishing in the lake towards the end of last season. I had caught a few small tench when my float ran off again. I struck and to my astonishment

I hooked a beautiful *golden* tench which is coloured as brightly as a goldfish but has black spots along its side. It was about 4 inches long and could not have been one of the original fish I put in from Leney in 1951.

The tench from that lot are now about the 2 and 3lb mark and give a grand account of themselves when hooked. They do not fight with the dash of the carp, but they tend to go deep and fight gamely. I would say that a big tench fights as well as a big carp and with just as much dogged power, but he will not make the same long, wild dashes. They have a habit, too, of standing on their noses on the bed of the pond when they feel the hook and trying to rub it out. This gives a curious thrumming sensation to the taut line.

I have found that in the lake the best time for tench is just after sunrise on a summer's morning when the surface of the pool is 'smoking' mist. I have caught all my best tench at such times, including the six pounder which came from the upper reservoir at Welford in Northamptonshire, which is a grand tench water and deserves to be better known than it is. I am sure it holds some 12lb tench. I have been broken there by a tench which I am certain was a record, which, by the way, stands at 8lb 8oz.

Late evening is also excellent, just when the bats are out and it becomes difficult to see your float, but the fish go off feed after sun-down.

I have known a huge bag of tench landed during the blazing noon-day hours, but this was when heavy ground-baiting with the well-known recipe of 'brewer's grains and bullock's blood' had been employed. There is no doubt that ground-baiting for tench is very necessary (as it is for carp) if you want to ensure continual sport.

I am not sure that I approve of huge bags of coarse fish. They are the dream of many a match fisherman but I prefer the odd biggish fish caught at edge of dark or in the milky mists of a July dawn. When feeding, tench do not stir up so much mud as carp, but the tell-tale 'needle bubbles' will betray where they are busy and, as they usually go about in shoals, you can trace these bubbles moving across the chosen swim. I have sometimes seen tench bubbles close to the boat when I have been anchored off the island and have dropped worms in amongst them to be taken right away.

If there are any bulrushes in a pool you may be sure that tench will be in the vicinity. This is certainly so in my lake and the same applies elsewhere. You will not need to cast so far as for carp, and tench seem on the whole less fearful of the suspicious shadow of a boat.

You can have lively fun fishing for tench with a small 8 foot split-cane rod and a 3lb B.S. line, but in the Wood Pool there is always the uneasy feeling that one of the giant carp will come along and seize the bunch of appetising worms. Then you might finish up with a smashed rod as I did at the end of last season.

The sexes of tench may be easily identified by the spoon-shaped pectoral fins of the male which is the more heavily built of the pair. On the table, tench are quite excellent but I rate them just a little lower than the mirror carp as they are inclined to have a muddy flavour. The flesh has a pale golden hue.

So far I have caught no large tench in the pool and I do not expect to do so for another ten years. Unfortunately, as they have bred so freely they may never reach a large size. The great merit of tench (and the same applies to carp) is that they can be introduced into quite small ponds; deep water is not entirely necessary to their well-being.

Many little field ponds, if stocked with tench, can provide a lot of pleasure and I wish angling clubs would view this fine sporting fish with greater favour. In the hand, tench appear to be slimy but they have not the disgusting greyish slime of the bream. Their scales are like those of the game fish, neat and soft, indeed they are more like trout than any other species of so-called 'coarse' fish.

One merit of tench in a garden pond is that they become very tame and can be taught to take worms from the fingers. The tamest of all coarse fish is the perch. They can be made to follow one round a pool like a dog and almost leap out to take worms. When I had a few perch in my garden pond they would come up and suck my fingers, goggling at me like a Pekingese in the most comical fashion. I found them most endearing creatures. However large tench may grow, there is not that feeling of awe when fishing for them which one experiences when fishing for giant carp.

The carp in the Wood Pool will never attain the proportions of the Redmire specimens. To grow to such a size they need very deep water as well as shallows. But I am confident that my fish will get into the 20lb category. The tench may become six pounders, but I doubt it. Even a 3lb tench is worth catching, and well worth eating, too, if you are so minded.

CHAPTER NINE

The Little Summer of St Luke

It is fitting that I bring this little book to an end on an October day. As always, about the middle of the month, when we get what the country people call the Little Summer of St Luke, these mellow warm days bring the carp on the rove for the last time. They are like the red admiral butterflies which are just now having a last fling on the great carmine and lilac trusses of the Michaelmas daisies along my herbaceous borders.

The carp, more than any of our fresh-water coarse fish, is a sun lover. By October's end they have tucked themselves up in the mud. Sometimes during the cold months when the pond is clear I can see them below in the shallower water, motionless like old drowned bottles and very much the same colour.

It is true there have been times in winter when carp have been caught, during exceptionally mild December days;

indeed, I have talked with a man who caught a 4lb mirror on Boxing Day, but this is very unusual.

Come then for a last voyage on this golden afternoon, of 15th October, 1957.

The path through the old ironstone workings is even more grown up. Huge barriers of briar have appeared, encroaching on the half-hidden track, the leaves are a hundred delicate tints from bronze and rose, to palest yellow and tenderest green.

Alas! The days of this lovely wilderness are numbered. Why is it that all the wild places are being 'tidied up' and improved by the busy-bodies with town minds who wish all waste lands to be cleared and levelled? Already surveyors are busy with their painted rods and within a month or so this beautiful paradise, where I have had so many happy times, will be bull-dozed flat and all the hawthorns will be uprooted; all will be nice and tidy!

From behind one of the briar bushes, where the long brittle 'lion' grass is now ashen ochre, there starts up, suddenly, a magnificent cock pheasant. Maybe he had been feeding on the blackberries, for the bushes are still thick with ripe fruit.

Mick, the black retriever, is at my heels and instead of a rod I carry my gun. This favourite weapon was originally built for a titled dame and is beautifully balanced and light. It must be forty years old at least. I had a pair of new barrels fitted a couple of years back which cost almost as much as the original gun complete.

The resplendent bird, 'cocking' hysterically, is driving upwards on his rounded wings. It is a shot which many good marksmen often miss, for the speed and rise are deceptive. But as the shot rings out the bird falls headlong, killed instantly in flight. It falls down into the 'lion' grass and one richly patterned feather floats idly after like an autumn leaf.

Mick has meanwhile stood like an ebony statue. He is waiting for me to send him on for the retrieve. He has turned his head a little looking at me out of the corner of his eye. I barely murmur 'hie lost' when he is gone with one black panther bound, over the coloured briars, away into the ashen grass. A moment's bustle, the glimpse of a feathering tail-tip, and he is coming back with the dead pheasant in his mouth. I take it from him and lay it on the bleached grass where the sun shines.

At such moments one cannot help considering what a wrong headed system it is that life should feed on life, that we sportsmen should enjoy shooting and fishing! If this bird had not been very good to eat I should not have taken its life, but the hunting instinct is strong within most men and, because it is natural that this should be so, all is well.

Nobody has described the plumage of the pheasant better than Ruskin who had an eye for such things. He says that in most specimens the plumage spots are 'more variegated, or inlaid as in a Byzantine pavement, deepening into imperial purple and azure, and lighting with the lustre of innumerable eyes'. Well said, Master Ruskin, well said!

At my shot some grey wood pigeons have been startled from the oaks over the tall hawthorns, others arrow hither and thither over the fir crests towards the pool.

The black poplars on the waterside are now a lovely shade of yellow, they are already thinning so that one can see the sweep of the branches. I can hear the mallard now, quacking in alarm. They too have heard that single shot ringing and echoing on the still gossamer air.

Soon I am walking under the oaks and can smell the rich, almost animal smell of the fallen leaves. It is the tannin perhaps which gives the oak woods their peculiar aroma. Among the thick green leaves as I pass under I can see the rich clusters of pale acorns, shaped like the helmets of Norman knights. They are arranged among the boldly serrated leaves in such a pleasing fashion, giving one a sense of exquisite design. No small wonder that the ancient craftsmen carvers delighted in portraying oak leaves and acorns on the old bench-ends and silvery grey stone capitals in country churches.

Most of the oak leaves, even at this late date (15th October), are still richly green. It is only the terminal branches which bear the tinted leaves, burned by a frost we had a week ago, a frost which stripped the limes in the park.

This strong scent of fallen oak leaves is with me until I climb the fence and step out into the little moist strip of 'meadow slip' which separates the wood from the pool. Here the grass has been uncut all summer. It is long, green, and dew wet. This 'strip meadow' never sees the sun save in coins of light which penetrate the belt of oaks.

There is a fallen willow just here, where I step into the sward. It grows on the bank of the pool, on the artificial bankment to be exact, and last winter half of it broke away to form a natural bridge which spans the brook. It grows just on the bend where the stream sweeps round and where there is a deepish pool. I have time and again placed a plank just here to span the brook but have been too lazy to anchor it. Every high flood has washed it away.

Now there is no need for a bridge because the willow has provided me with a permanent foot-way. The half of the willow which has fallen in the meadow still retains its slender yellowing leaves. The grass has grown up long and tall through the branches, for the cattle were unable to browse it down.

There was a wasps' nest here earlier in the summer and I took the nest and used the grubs for fishing. Few coarse fish can resist a nice fat white wasp grub straight from the comb.

Mick immediately becomes interested in this long dead tangle. His black stern wags, his big head is thrust in among the tall whippy twigs. I expect a pheasant to be there. Maybe it had been gathering acorns in the ditch under the oaks and heard us coming through the wood.

A moment later there is a bustle; out pops a rabbit. The gun, which was at the ready, is lowered, for the rabbit is part of my sporting life. All my memories of shooting as a boy are bound up with this humble little rascal in hodden grey.

I do not fire as it scuttles along the bank, diving with a flourish of its white scut into the thick rusty tangle of the meadow-sweet which covers all the lower flat of the meadow below the pool embankment. Quite like old times! As it runs it disturbs the bullfinch families feeding on the meadow-sweet seed of which these pretty, shy finches are very fond. They dip away into the wood, their diminutive white rumps moving with switchback flight.

Mick turns his head full round and looks at me with astonishment. His mystification is comical. 'Why the hell didn't your fire?' he seems to ask.

Perhaps one day I shall shoot a rabbit again, I hope so, but now I guard these gallant survivors. They are stub rabbits. The powers that be cannot gas them for they have no holes; nothing short of another dose of 'myxa' will kill them and as there are still so few this is unlikely. Myxa kills when the rabbit population becomes overcrowded, then many of the survivors become immune. I unload the gun, slipping the two heavy orange cases into my jacket pocket. Steadying myself by a handy branch I walk across the trunk, jumping down on the grass of the bank. Mick plunges into the brook behind and comes scrambling at my heels, stopping to shake the water out of his coat.

I top the bank and look straight across the polished surface of the pond. Being almost on an eye-level with the water it is like looking along the brimming surface of a full glass. The hazy sun shining away over the wood on the left makes a gauzy veil of light which softens the distant island trees.

All along the woodside the trees show a multitude of colours, ambers and yellows, dark-green and light-greens, and in one or two places, the burning pink flames of dying maple leaves.

There is also the high, gaunt dead tree where the herons love to sit to digest their heavy meals, and where the pigeons always perch when they first come in on the evening flight.

The shining surface of the pool is broken and starred by flashes of light where three mallard are swimming slowly about, quite unaware I am watching them from the embankment. Perhaps they know I will not harm them. There are two fine drakes in all their glory of winter kit, and one drab duck. As I watch them a fish leaps up, rising clear of the surface and falling back with a loud splash. The disturbance causes widening rings which wheel outwards breaking up their reflections. I know that if I watch he will most likely jump again, and so he does, a moment later, but many yards closer to the island where I caught my big fish. Then another jumps, this time some distance off, right against the edge of the reeds along the north side and not far from the bulrush beds. This is an even bigger fish and it looks golden primrose in the limpid light, possibly a ten pounder.

In a very short time they will jump no more. I doubt if they would look at a bait even now, though they might do so in the warmest part of the day.

I make my way slowly round to the boat-house, brushing through the dew-wet, dead, meadow-sweet and the small briars. I unlock the door and enter the cold gloom which smells of tar and far-away sea harbours.

Mick does not like the boat-house. He will not enter unless I whistle him in.

I step down into the boat, leaving the gun and game bag on the staging for I never shoot on the lake. Mick enters the boat with his usual great reluctance.

Winter seems here, already, in the boat-house, it is so sunless and chill. No weaving flies now, just above the surface of the water, no scolding sedge warblers this afternoon! No 'flames of June'.

A stroke of the oar and we are entering Congo Channel. How different from that other day last summer! The sedges have gone rusty at their sharp tips, everywhere the reed beds are dying.

Surprisingly, a furrow cleaves the channel ahead as a smallish fish hurries back towards the main lake. It is late for them to be so far up here; perhaps it was on a voyage of discovery and was intending to reach the deep weedy hole by the boat-house.

Mallards rise at almost every bend of the channel, quacking loudly, the soft sunlight shining on their metallic bottle-green necks. They quack vigorously as they rise, the bright water winks from their hanging orange-tinted paddles.

Now we are in the open pools between the sedges, opposite where the cattle come to drink on summers' evenings, and where at times, one may see a good fish cruising in the sunlit amber shallows.

Then comes the sharp turn by the willow bush which is now almost bare, then turn right again for the island and the deeper water. A few more strokes and we are past the shadowed island where, like the boat-house interior, winter seems already come. We are gliding out into the sunlit main lake, watching the bunches of mallard packing tight in the sky and making off northwards for the distant Nene valley. There are dead leaves floating on the still water, leaves from the willows, from the birches, alders, and limes. They form close-patterned rafts which gently part asunder as the boat moves onwards.

Everywhere a misty loveliness which veils the line of woods, giving to even the most vivid autumn tints a silvery quality. Though it is not yet four o'clock there is already little warmth in the sun and, as we glide softly in the lee of the big bulrush beds, the wood pigeons are streaming in to roost. Party after party comes over, their reflections moving across the still mirror.

It was just about here I had my big catches of tench and carp last July. I always came back with half-a-dozen good 'breakfast' mirrors and only once, during the summer, did I return with an empty creel.

As I look across to the willow bush on the south bank one more carp leaps up, a fish of 4lb perhaps, and like the other we saw earlier, it appears a rosy gold in the soft light. Splash!

It falls back into the pond and the ripples widen and widen until they reach the boat. Maybe it will be the last fish we shall see jump this season, for angling in Wood Pool is over now. A sad thought. Yet, looking at this beautiful calm lake so serene in this mellow light, I have a feeling of great satisfaction. A few years back it was a dead water, with half the interest it now holds.

Very soon now the leaves will all have fallen, later the thick grey ice will roof this polished mirror from bank to bank. But summer days will come again and with them I hope many a quiet hour, waiting for the first stir of the painted float as one of the grandfathers makes up his mind to run.

Simple pleasures maybe, but very real ones, which seem all the more precious in these restless, modern days.